POPULAR SONGS
HAL LEONARD
STUDENT PIANO LIBRARY

INTERMEDIATE LEVEL

T0048282

Jerome Kern Classics

FOR PIANO SOLO

ARRANGED BY EUGÉNIE ROCHEROLLE

In loving memory of my parents, Gustave J. Ricau, Jr. and Katherine Schlegel Ricau, who, with their combined talents of voice and piano, filled my young years with the music of Jerome Kern.

CONTENTS

Edited by J. Mark Baker

ISBN 978-0-634-09081-3

HAL•LEONARD®
CORPORATION
7777 W. BLUEMOUND RD. P.O. BOX 13819 MILWAUKEE, WI 53213

Visit Hal Leonard Online at
www.halleonard.com

Jerome David Kern (1885-1945) wrote some of the greatest music in the history of Broadway and Hollywood. He received his first musical instruction from his mother, who taught him to play the piano. As a teenager, Kern studied harmony, theory, and piano at the New York College of Music, and later continued his training at the famous Heidelburg Conservatory in Germany.

Born a generation after Victor Herbert and a generation before Richard Rodgers, Kern's musical style provides a bridge between the older European operetta and the newer American musical comedy. His exhaustive knowledge of stagecraft made it possible for him to unite the mastery of lyrical song with the theatrical demands of plot and character motivation to give birth to the American musical play.

Show Boat (1927), Kern's most important work, is often reckoned the most influential Broadway musical of all time because it led composers of Broadway plays to become aware of a musically and dramatically integrated production, rather than simply writing Tin Pan Alley songs for interpolation. Four of its songs, all of which are an essential part of the characterization and story, are included in this collection: "Bill," "Can't Help Lovin' Dat Man," "Make Believe," and " Ol' Man River."

Kern's songs are distinguished by sophisticated lyrics, conversational phrasing, and the use of varied, incisive rhythms. "I've Told Ev'ry Little Star," from *Music in the Air* (1932), demonstrates Kern's genius for combining changing rhythmic patterns with elegantly suspended vocal lines. "Who?" from *Sunny* (1925), juxtaposes long notes with small groups of fast notes, a characteristic of some of his finest, most facile melodies.

Several of Kern's stage works were adapted for the screen, beginning with *Roberta* (1933, filmed 1935), which featured "Smoke Gets In Your Eyes." In the mid-1930s, Kern began composing original film scores. The most famous of these was *Swing Time* (1936), in which Fred Astaire sings "The Way You Look Tonight" to Ginger Rogers. After *Very Warm for May* (1939), which included one of Kern's best songs, "All The Things You Are," flopped on Broadway, Kern moved to Hollywood and wrote exclusively for the movies. For these he produced some of his most seasoned songs, including "The Last Time I Saw Paris," which won an Academy Award when it was used in *Lady, Be Good* (1941).

With nearly 1000 songs in over 100 stage works, Jerome Kern is quite possibly America's most prolific theatre composer. His memorable melodies have brought joy to generations of music lovers the world over. May you find enjoyment in playing these arrangements of ten of his most beloved works.

Bill

from SHOW BOAT

Music by JEROME KERN
Words by P.G. WODEHOUSE and OSCAR HAMMERSTEIN II
Arranged by Eugénie Rocherolle

Moderately fast (♩ = 96)

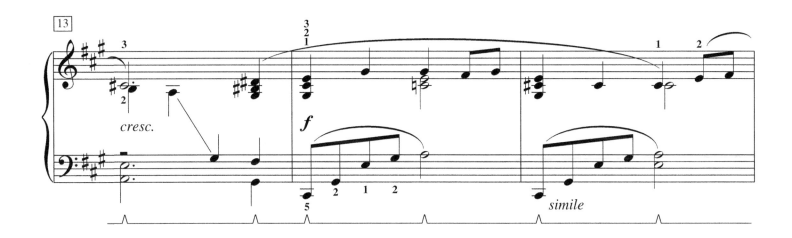

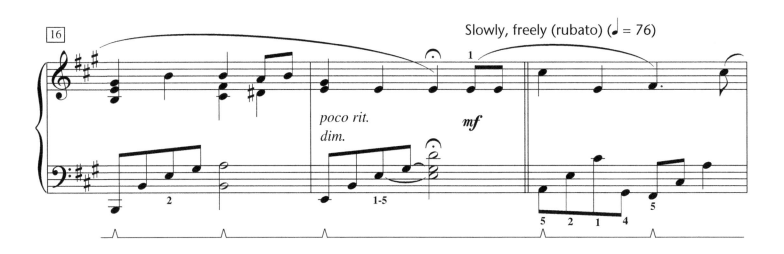

Slowly, freely (rubato) (♩ = 76)

poco rit.
dim.

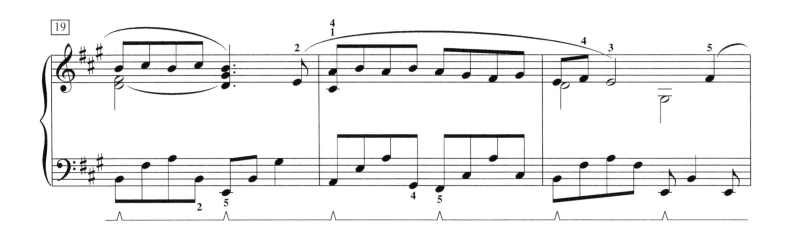

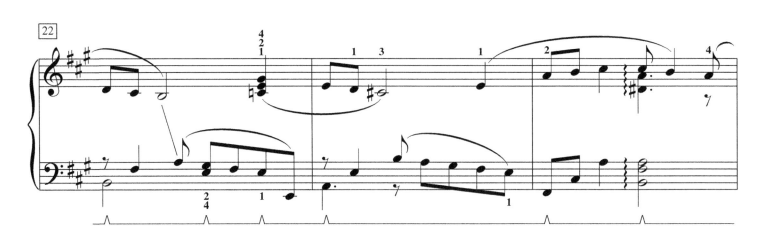

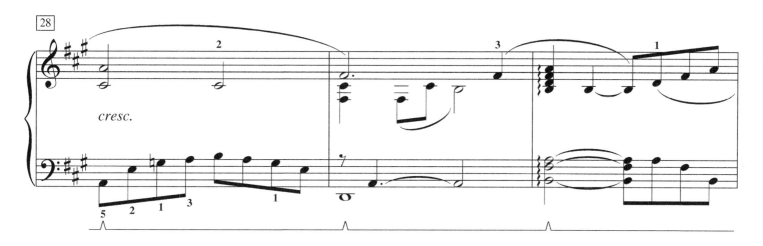

(1'51")

All The Things You Are

from VERY WARM FOR MAY

Lyrics by OSCAR HAMMERSTEIN II
Music by JEROME KERN
Arranged by Eugénie Rocherolle

Moderately (♩ = 63)

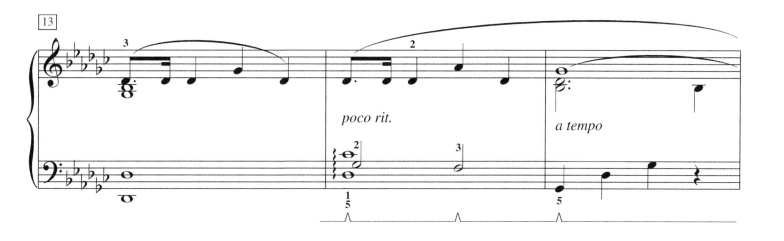

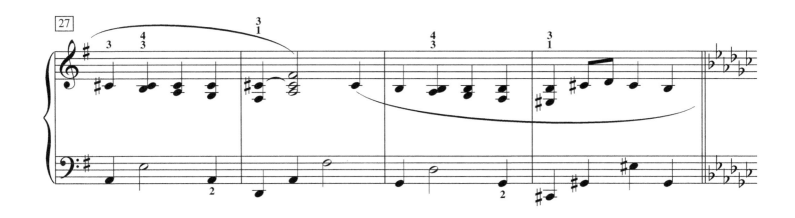

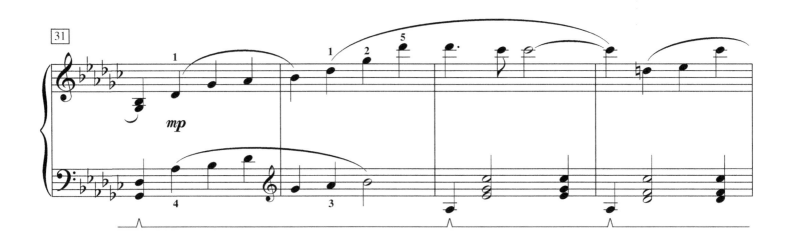

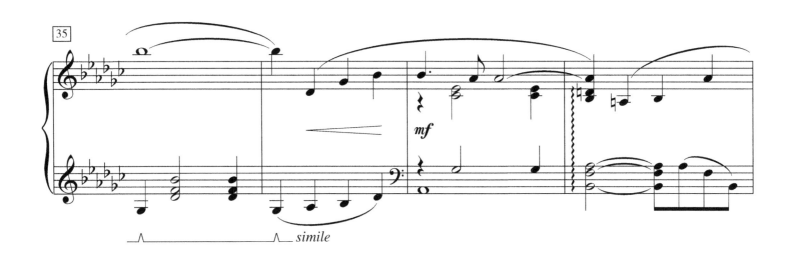

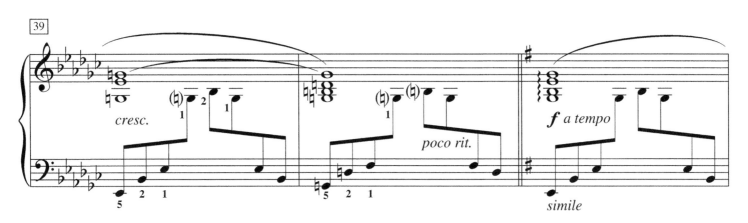

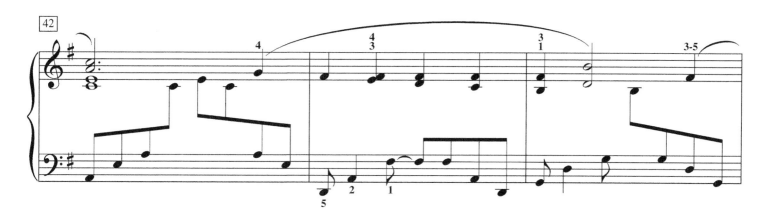

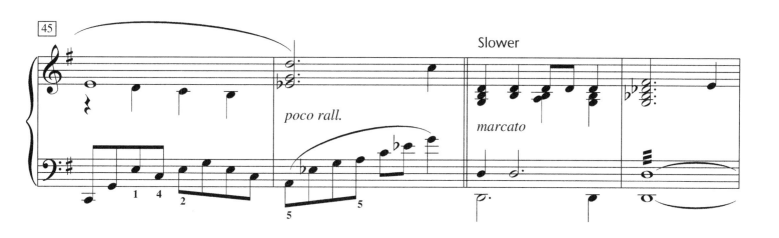

(1'50")

Can't Help Lovin' Dat Man

from SHOW BOAT

Lyrics by OSCAR HAMMERSTEIN II
Music by JEROME KERN
Arranged by Eugénie Rocherolle

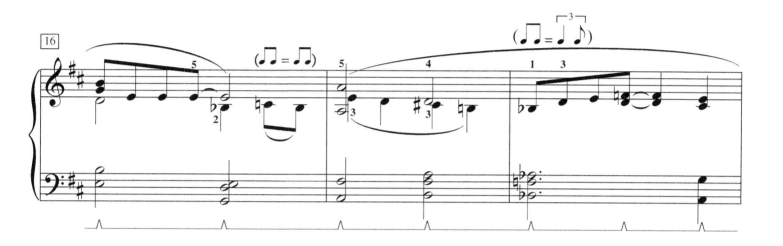

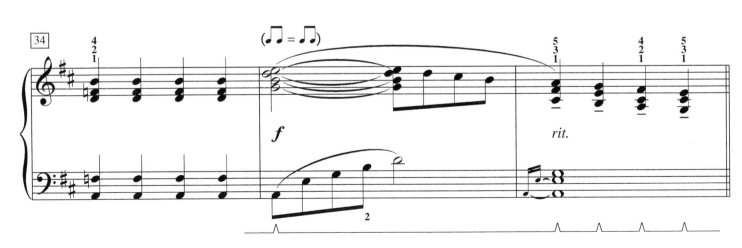

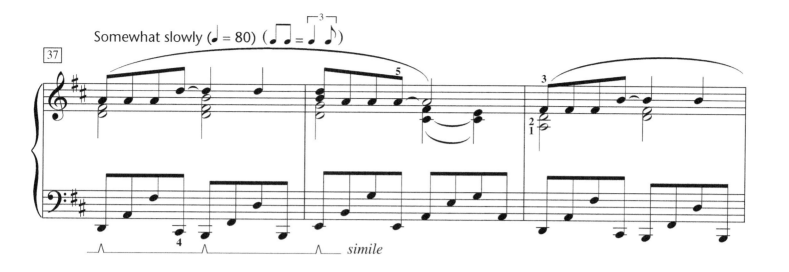

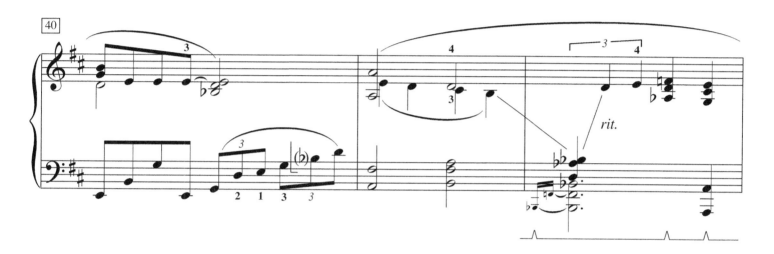

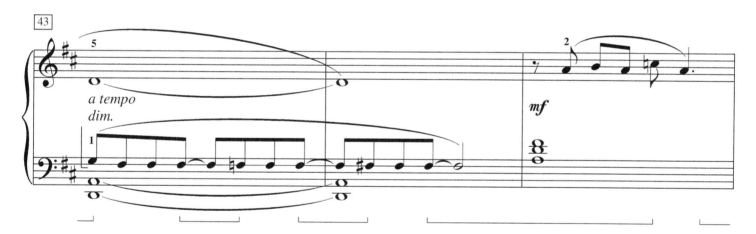

(2'18")

I've Told Ev'ry Little Star

from MUSIC IN THE AIR

Lyrics by OSCAR HAMMERSTEIN II
Music by JEROME KERN
Arranged by Eugénie Rocherolle

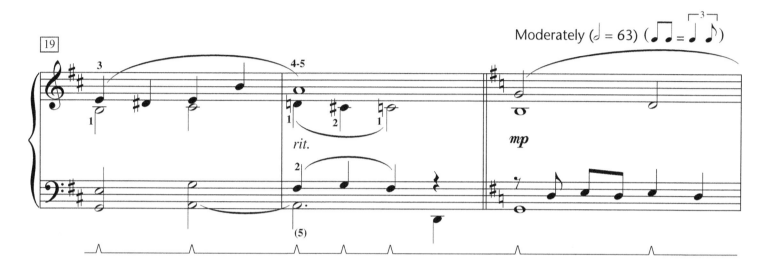

Moderately (♩ = 63) (♪♪ = ♩♪³)

rit.

mp

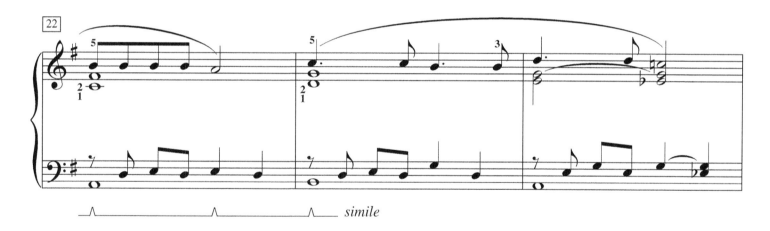

simile

simile

A bit faster (♩ = 72)

_mf_

16

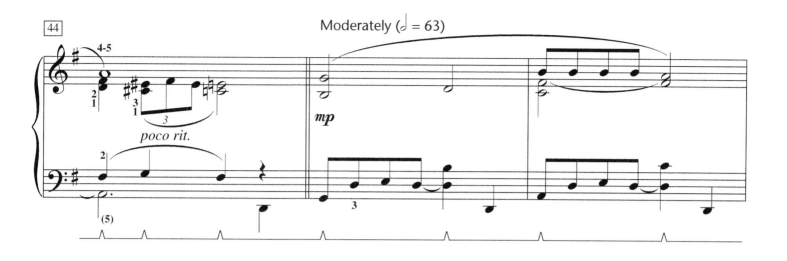

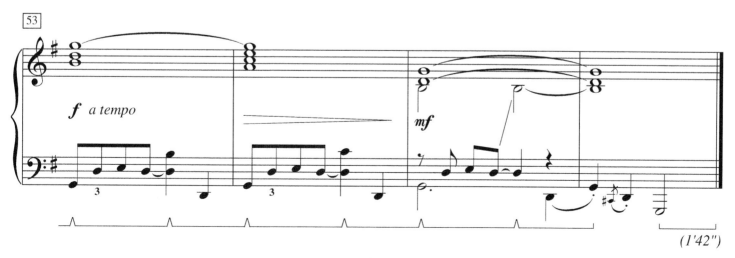

The Last Time I Saw Paris

from LADY, BE GOOD

Lyrics by OSCAR HAMMERSTEIN II
Music by JEROME KERN
Arranged by Eugénie Rocherolle

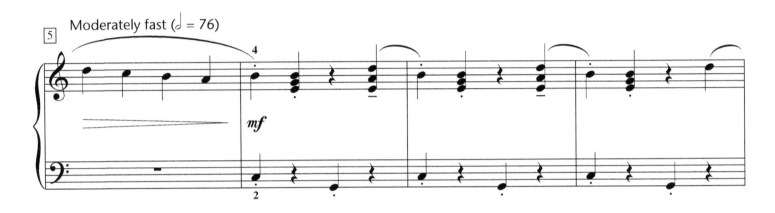

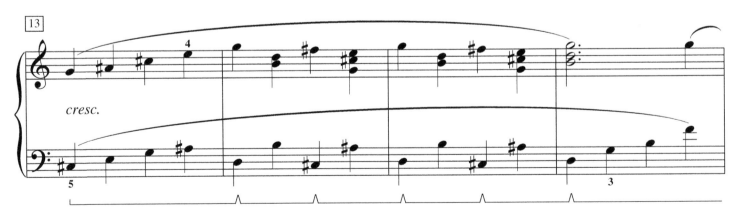

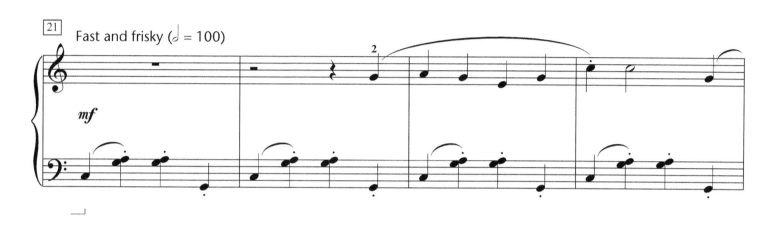

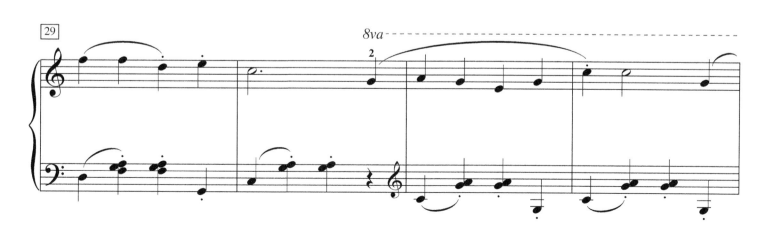

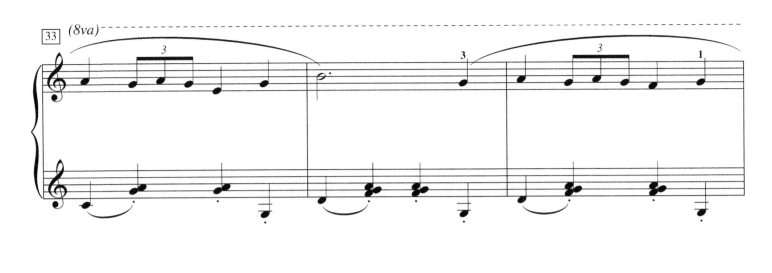

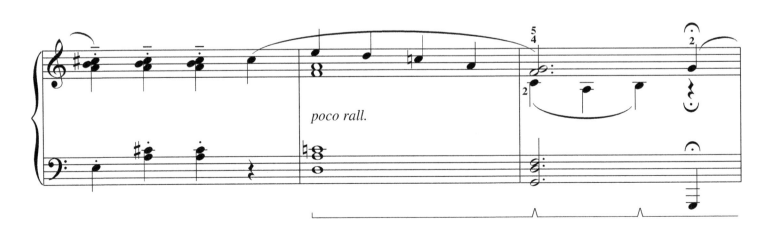

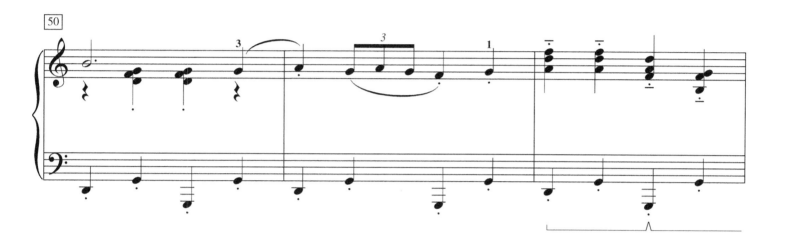

(1'23")

21

Make Believe

from SHOW BOAT

Lyrics by OSCAR HAMMERSTEIN II
Music by JEROME KERN
Arranged by Eugénie Rocherolle

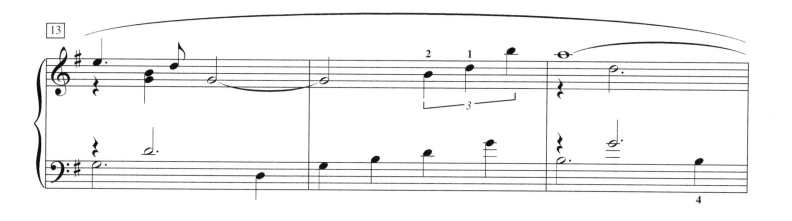

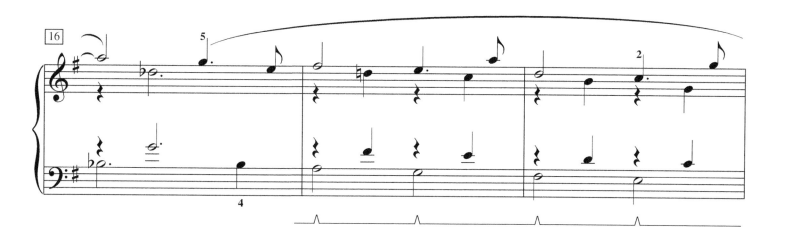

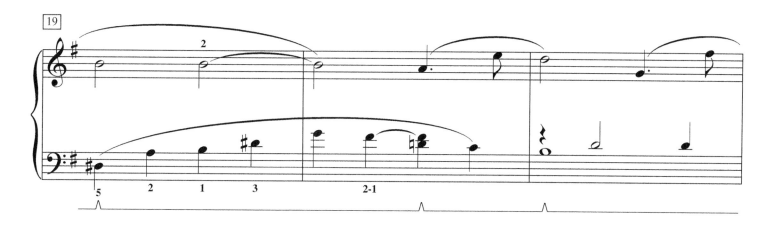

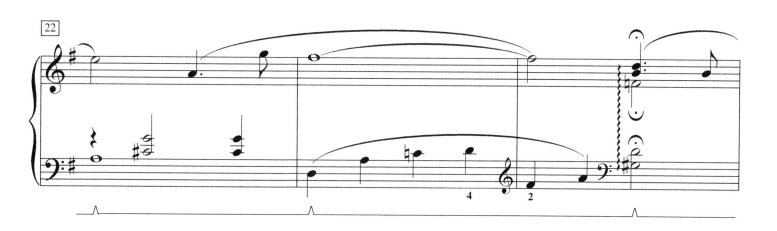

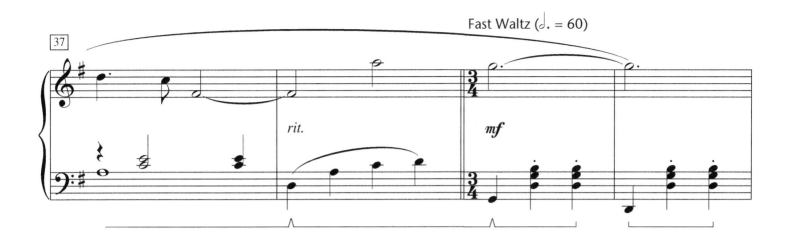

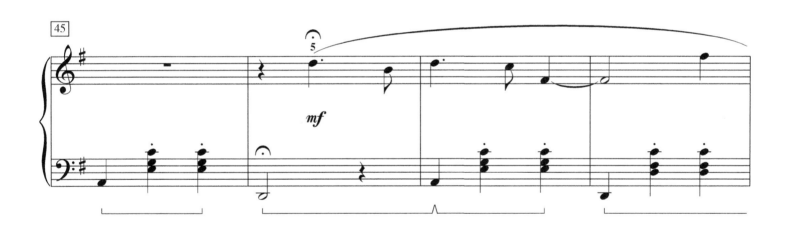

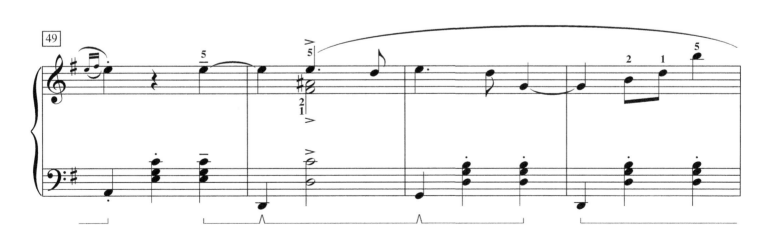

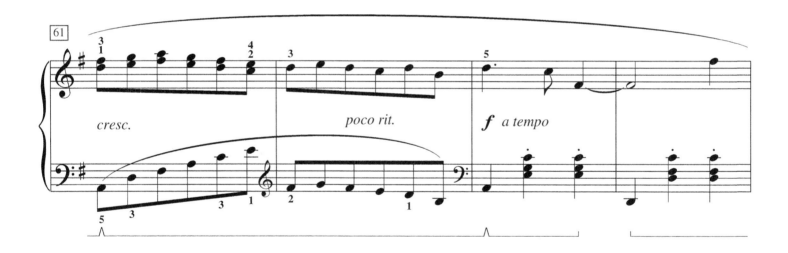

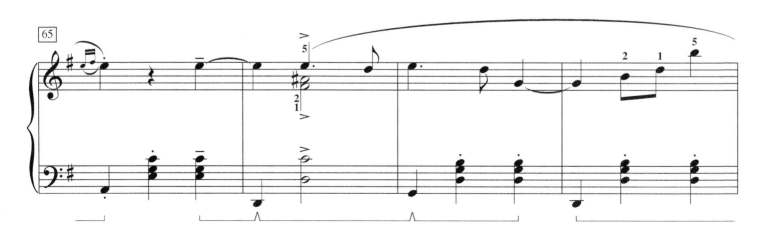

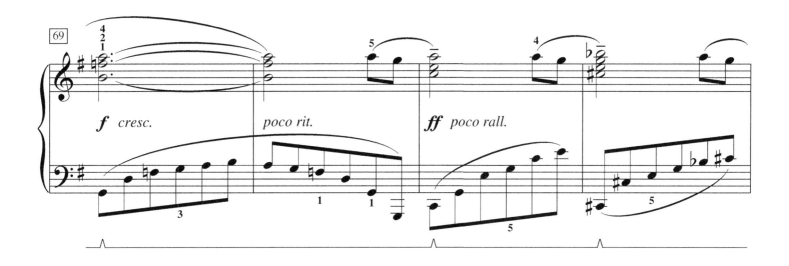

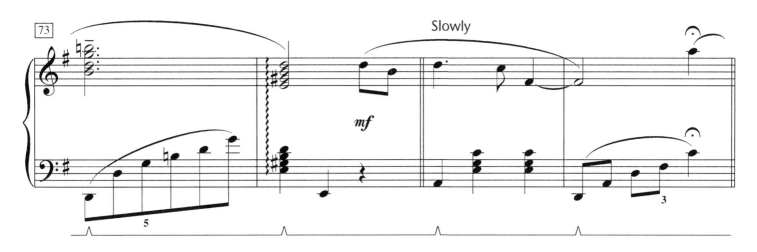

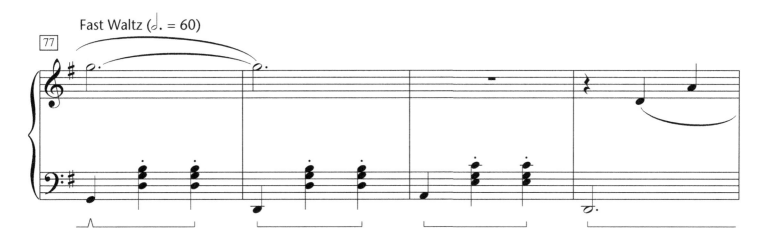

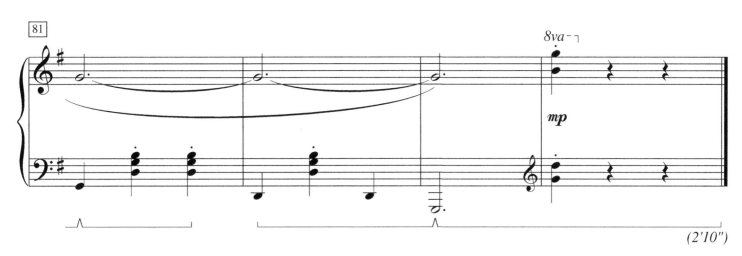

(2'10")

Ol' Man River

from SHOW BOAT

Lyrics by OSCAR HAMMERSTEIN II
Music by JEROME KERN
Arranged by Eugénie Rocherolle

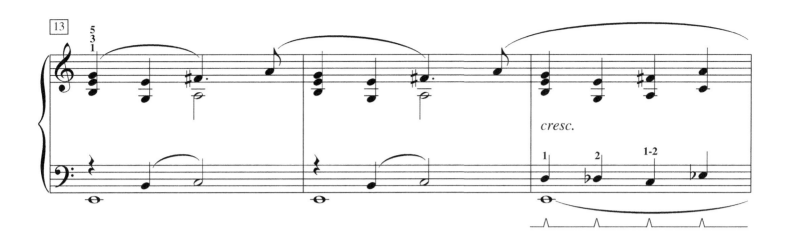

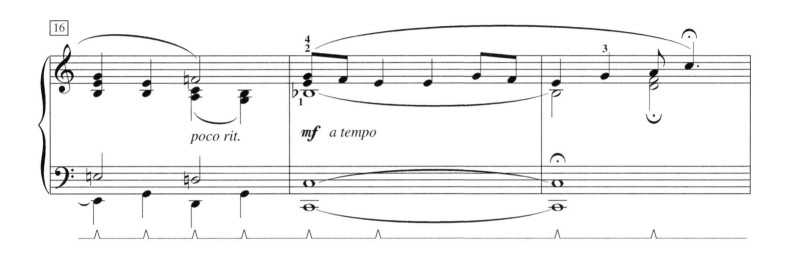

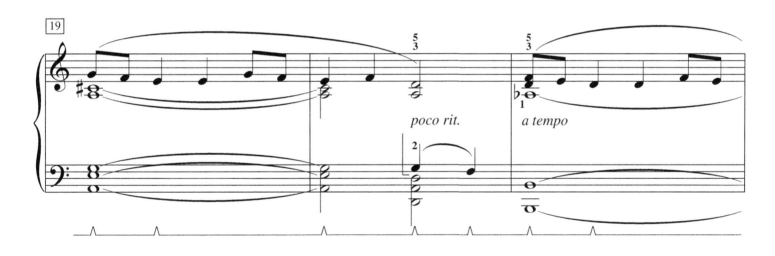

Moderately slow, with feeling (♩ = 76)

(2'36")

Smoke Gets In Your Eyes

from ROBERTA

Words by OTTO HARBACH
Music by JEROME KERN
Arranged by Eugénie Rocherolle

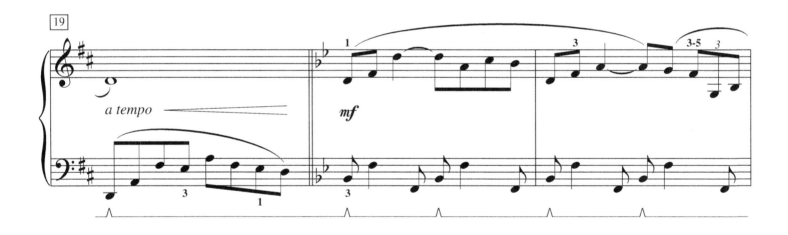

(1'43")

Who?

from SUNNY

Lyrics by OTTO HARBACH and OSCAR HAMMERSTEIN II
Music by JEROME KERN
Arranged by Eugénie Rocherolle

Moderately (♩ = 84)

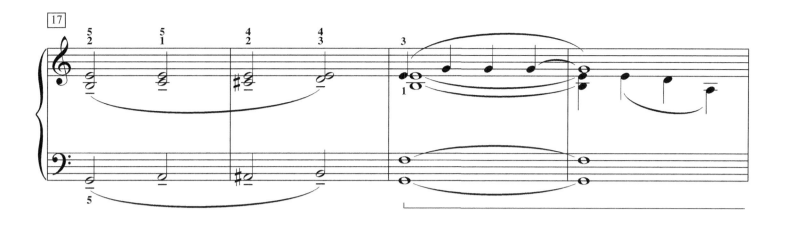

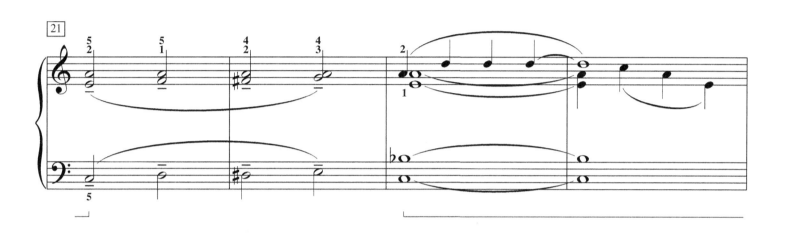

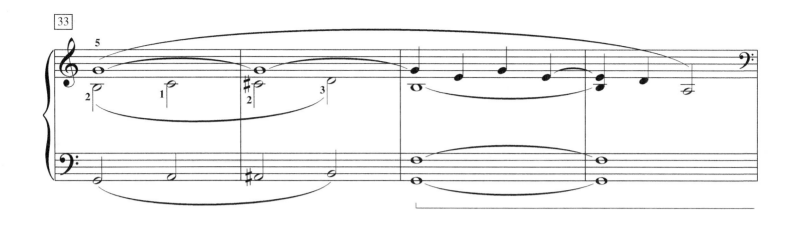

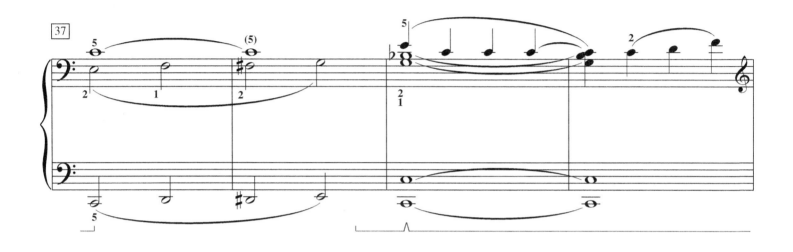

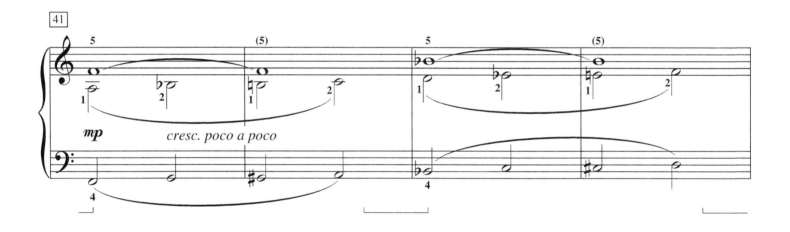

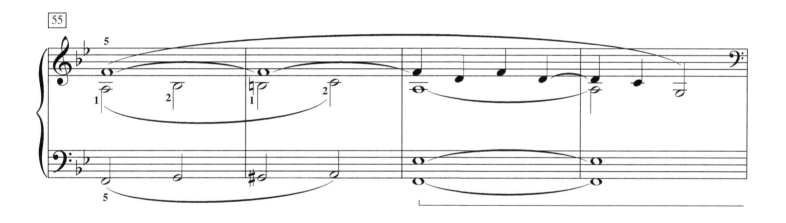

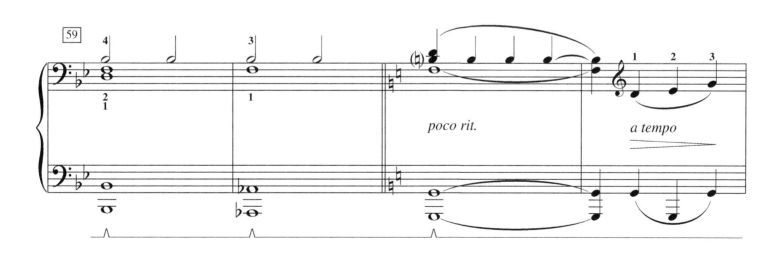

poco rit.

a tempo

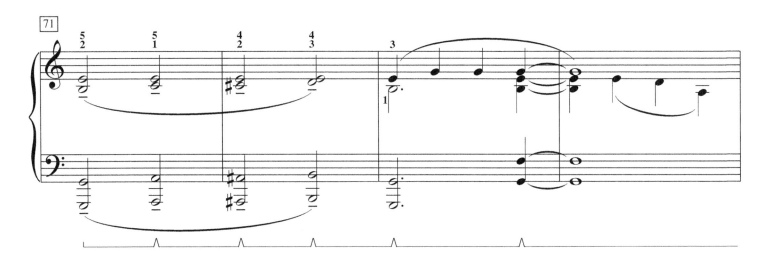

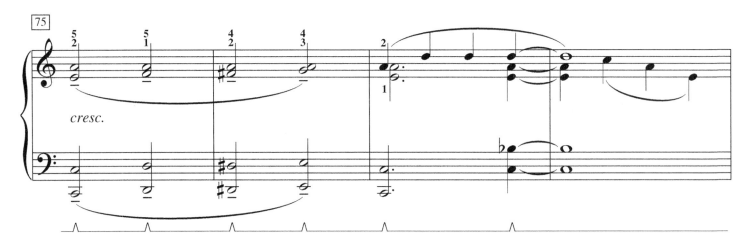

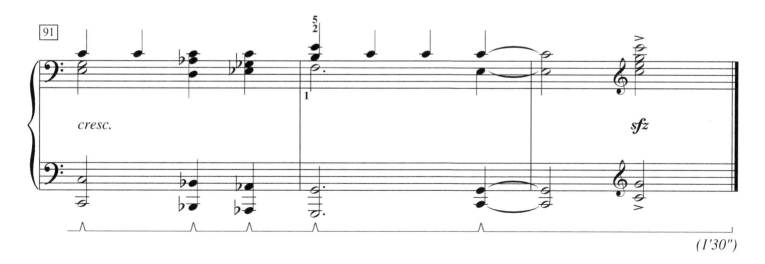

(1'30")

41

The Way You Look Tonight

from SWING TIME

Words by DOROTHY FIELDS
Music by JEROME KERN
Arranged by Eugénie Rocherolle

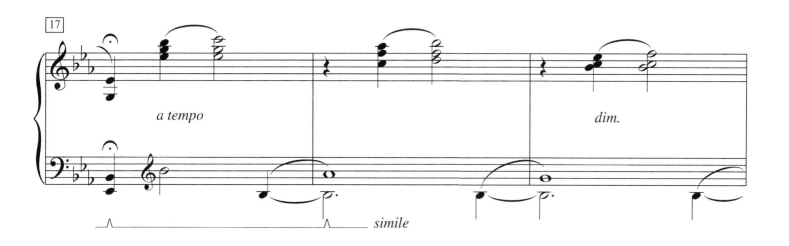

a tempo　　　　　　　　　　　　　　　　*dim.*

simile

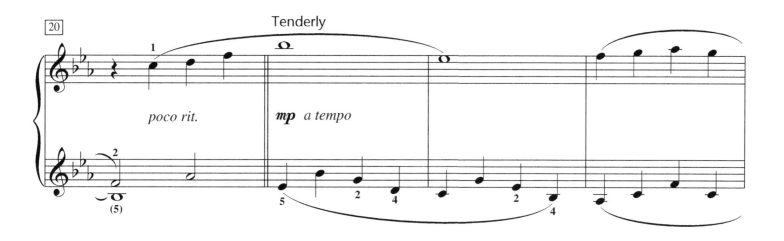

Tenderly

poco rit.　　　**mp** *a tempo*

(5)

poco cresc. e accel.

poco rit.　　　**mf** *a tempo*　　　　　　　　*dim.*

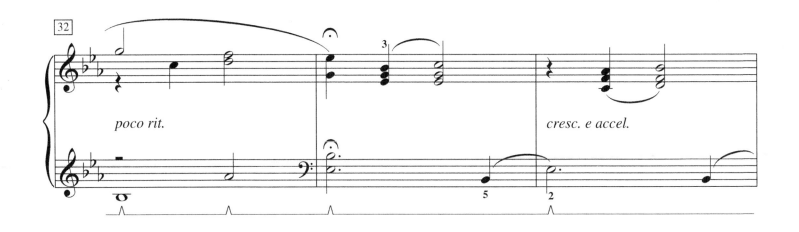

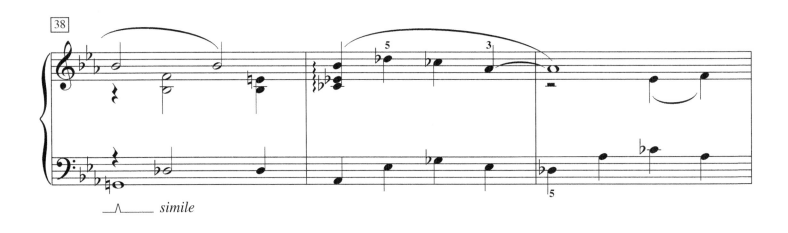

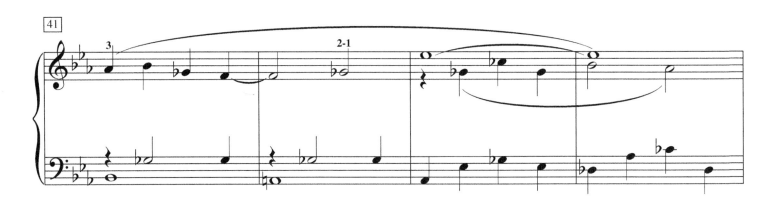

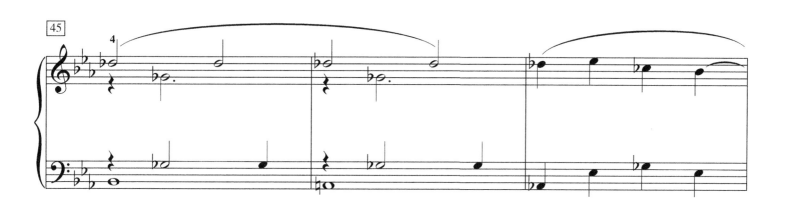

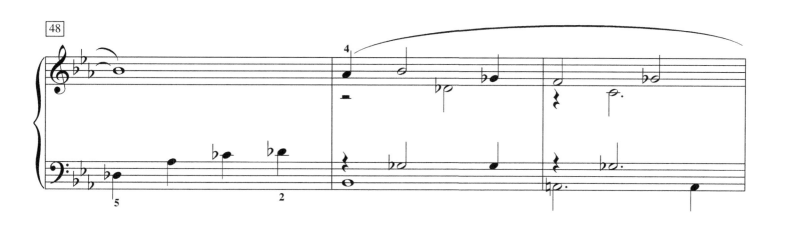

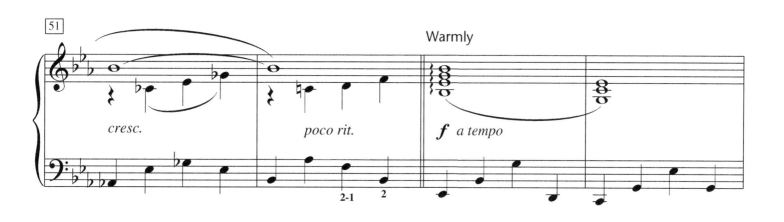

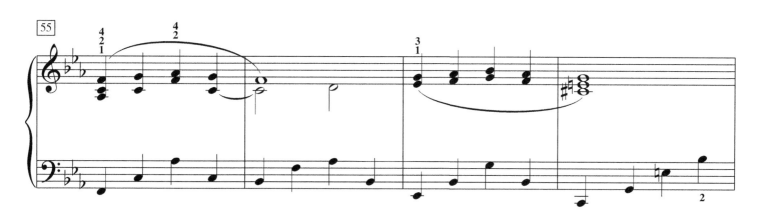

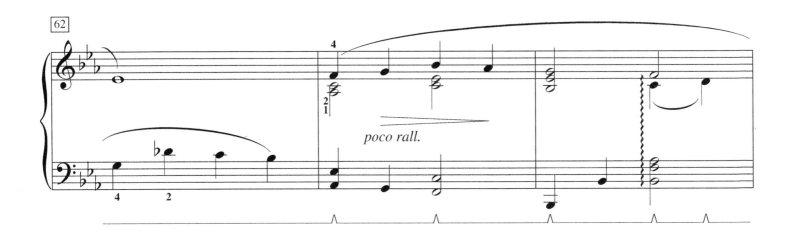

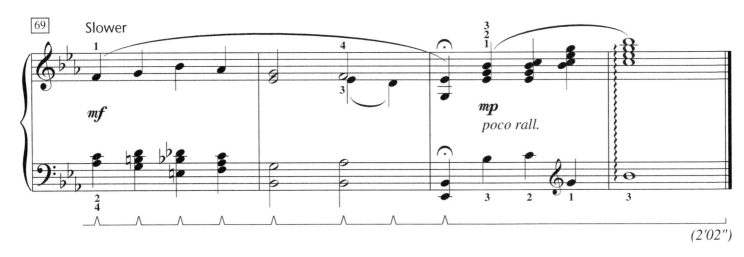

(2'02")

COMPOSER SHOWCASE
HAL LEONARD STUDENT PIANO LIBRARY

This series showcases great original piano music from our **Hal Leonard Student Piano Library** family of composers. Carefully graded for easy selection.

BILL BOYD

JAZZ BITS (AND PIECES)
Early Intermediate Level
00290312 11 Solos............................$7.99

JAZZ DELIGHTS
Intermediate Level
00240435 11 Solos............................$8.99

JAZZ FEST
Intermediate Level
00240436 10 Solos............................$8.99

JAZZ PRELIMS
Early Elementary Level
00290032 12 Solos............................$7.99

JAZZ SKETCHES
Intermediate Level
00220001 8 Solos............................$8.99

JAZZ STARTERS
Elementary Level
00290425 10 Solos............................$7.99

JAZZ STARTERS II
Late Elementary Level
00290434 11 Solos............................$7.99

JAZZ STARTERS III
Late Elementary Level
00290465 12 Solos............................$8.99

THINK JAZZ!
Early Intermediate Level
00290417 Method Book.........................$12.99

TONY CARAMIA

JAZZ MOODS
Intermediate Level
00296728 8 Solos............................$6.95

SUITE DREAMS
Intermediate Level
00296775 4 Solos............................$6.99

SONDRA CLARK

THREE ODD METERS
Intermediate Level
00296472 3 Duets............................$6.95

MATTHEW EDWARDS

CONCERTO FOR YOUNG PIANISTS
FOR 2 PIANOS, FOUR HANDS
Intermediate Level Book/CD
00296356 3 Movements $19.99

CONCERTO NO. 2 IN G MAJOR
FOR 2 PIANOS, 4 HANDS
Intermediate Level Book/CD
00296670 3 Movements.........................$17.99

PHILLIP KEVEREN

MOUSE ON A MIRROR
Late Elementary Level
00296361 5 Solos............................$8.99

MUSICAL MOODS
Elementary/Late Elementary Level
00296714 7 Solos............................$6.99

SHIFTY-EYED BLUES
Late Elementary Level
00296374 5 Solos............................$7.99

CAROL KLOSE

THE BEST OF CAROL KLOSE
Early Intermediate to Late Intermediate Level
00146151 15 Solos...........................$12.99

CORAL REEF SUITE
Late Elementary Level
00296354 7 Solos............................$7.50

DESERT SUITE
Intermediate Level
00296667 6 Solos............................$7.99

FANCIFUL WALTZES
Early Intermediate Level
00296473 5 Solos............................$7.95

GARDEN TREASURES
Late Intermediate Level
00296787 5 Solos............................$8.50

ROMANTIC EXPRESSIONS
Intermediate/Late Intermediate Level
00296923 5 Solos............................$8.99

WATERCOLOR MINIATURES
Early Intermediate Level
00296848 7 Solos............................$7.99

JENNIFER LINN

AMERICAN IMPRESSIONS
Intermediate Level
00296471 6 Solos............................$8.99

ANIMALS HAVE FEELINGS TOO
Early Elementary/Elementary Level
00147789 8 Solos............................$8.99

CHRISTMAS IMPRESSIONS
Intermediate Level
00296706 8 Solos............................$8.99

JUST PINK
Elementary Level
00296722 9 Solos............................$8.99

LES PETITES IMAGES
Late Elementary Level
00296664 7 Solos............................$8.99

LES PETITES IMPRESSIONS
Intermediate Level
00296355 6 Solos............................$7.99

REFLECTIONS
Late Intermediate Level
00296843 5 Solos............................$8.99

TALES OF MYSTERY
Intermediate Level
00296769 6 Solos............................$8.99

LYNDA LYBECK-ROBINSON

ALASKA SKETCHES
Early Intermediate Level
00119637 8 Solos............................$7.99

AN AWESOME ADVENTURE
Late Elementary Level
00137563......................................$7.99

FOR THE BIRDS
Early Intermediate/Intermediate Level
00237078 ....$8.99

WHISPERING WOODS
Late Elementary Level
00275905 9 Solos............................$8.99

MONA REJINO

CIRCUS SUITE
Late Elementary Level
00296665 5 Solos............................$6.99

COLOR WHEEL
Early Intermediate Level
00201951 6 Solos............................$8.99

JUST FOR KIDS
Elementary Level
00296840 8 Solos............................$7.99

MERRY CHRISTMAS MEDLEYS
Intermediate Level
00296799 5 Solos............................$8.99

MINIATURES IN STYLE
Intermediate Level
00148088 6 Solos............................$8.99

PORTRAITS IN STYLE
Early Intermediate Level
00296507 6 Solos............................$8.99

EUGÉNIE ROCHEROLLE

CELEBRATION SUITE
Intermediate Level
00152724 3 Duets (1 Piano, 4 Hands)..............$8.99

**ENCANTOS ESPAÑOLES
(SPANISH DELIGHTS)**
Intermediate Level
00125451 6 Solos............................$8.99

JAMBALAYA
Intermediate Level
00296654 Ensemble (2 Pianos, 8 Hands)........$12.99

JAMBALAYA
Intermediate Level
00296725 Piano Duo (2 Pianos) $7.95

LITTLE BLUES CONCERTO
FOR 2 PIANOS, 4 HANDS
Early Intermediate Level
00142801 Piano Duo (2 Pianos, 4 Hands)........$12.99

TOUR FOR TWO
Late Elementary Level
00296832 6 Duets............................$7.99

TREASURES
Late Elementary/Early Intermediate Level
00296924 7 Solos............................$8.99

JEREMY SISKIND

BIG APPLE JAZZ
Intermediate Level
00278209 8 Solos............................$8.99

MYTHS AND MONSTERS
Late Elementary/Early Intermediate Level
00148148 9 Solos............................$7.99

CHRISTOS TSITSAROS

DANCES FROM AROUND THE WORLD
Early Intermediate Level
00296688 7 Solos............................$8.99

LYRIC BALLADS
Intermediate/Late Intermediate Level
00102404 6 Solos............................$8.99

POETIC MOMENTS
Intermediate Level
00296403 8 Solos............................$8.99

SEA DIARY
Early Intermediate Level
00253486 9 Solos............................$8.99

SONATINA HUMORESQUE
Late Intermediate Level
00296772 3 Movements $6.99

SONGS WITHOUT WORDS
Intermediate Level
00296506 9 Solos............................$9.99

THREE PRELUDES
Early Advanced Level
00130747 ....$8.99

THROUGHOUT THE YEAR
Late Elementary Level
00296723 12 Duets............................$6.95

ADDITIONAL COLLECTIONS

AT THE LAKE
by Elvina Pearce
Elementary/Late Elementary Level
00131642 10 Solos and Duets.........................$7.99

COUNTY RAGTIME FESTIVAL
by Fred Kern
Intermediate Level
00296882 7 Rags............................$7.99

LITTLE JAZZERS
by Jennifer Watts
Elementary/Late Elementary Level
00154573 Solos...............................8.99

PLAY THE BLUES!
by Luann Carman (Method Book)
Early Intermediate Level
00296357 10 Solos............................$9.99

Prices, contents, and availability subject
to change without notice.

HAL•LEONARD®

www.halleonard.com

POPULAR SONGS
HAL LEONARD STUDENT PIANO LIBRARY

The **Hal Leonard Student Piano Library** has great songs, and you will find all your favorites here: Disney classics, Broadway and movie favorites, and today's top hits. These graded collections are skillfully and imaginatively arranged for students and pianists at every level, from elementary solos with teacher accompaniments to sophisticated piano solos for the advancing pianist.

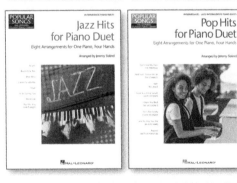

Adele
arr. Mona Rejino
00159590 Correlates with HLSPL Level 5..........$12.99

The Beatles
arr. Eugénie Rocherolle
00296649 Correlates with HLSPL Level 5..........$10.99

Irving Berlin Piano Duos
arr. Don Heitler and Jim Lyke
00296838 Correlates with HLSPL Level 5..........$14.99

Broadway Favorites
arr. Phillip Keveren
00279192 Correlates with HLSPL Level 4..........$12.99

Broadway Hits
arr. Carol Klose
00296650 Correlates with HLSPL Levels 4/5.......$8.99

Chart Hits
arr. Mona Rejino
00296710 Correlates with HLSPL Level 5...........$8.99

Christmas Cheer
arr. Phillip Keveren
00296616 Correlates with HLSPL Level 4............$8.99

Classic Christmas Favorites
arr. Jennifer & Mike Watts
00129582 Correlates with HLSPL Level 5............$9.99

Christmas Time Is Here
arr. Eugénie Rocherolle
00296614 Correlates with HLSPL Level 5............$8.99

Classic Joplin Rags
arr. Fred Kern
00296743 Correlates with HLSPL Level 5............$9.99

Classical Pop –
Lady Gaga Fugue & Other Pop Hits
arr. Giovanni Dettori
00296921 Correlates with HLSPL Level 5..........$12.99

Contemporary Movie Hits
arr. by Carol Klose, Jennifer Linn and Wendy Stevens
00296780 Correlates with HLSPL Level 5............$8.99

Contemporary Pop Hits
arr. Wendy Stevens
00296836 Correlates with HLSPL Level 3............$8.99

Country Favorites
arr. Mona Rejino
00296861 Correlates with HLSPL Level 5............$9.99

Current Hits
arr. Mona Rejino
00296768 Correlates with HLSPL Level 5............$8.99

Disney Favorites
arr. Phillip Keveren
00296647 Correlates with HLSPL Levels 3/4.......$9.99

Disney Film Favorites
arr. Mona Rejino
00296809 Correlates with HLSPL Level 5..........$10.99

Easy Christmas Duets
arr. Mona Rejino and Phillip Keveren
00237139 Correlates with HLSPL Level 3/4........$9.99

Easy Disney Duets
arr. Jennifer and Mike Watts
00243727 Correlates with HLSPL Level 4..........$12.99

Four Hands on Broadway
arr. Fred Kern
00146177 Correlates with HLSPL Level 5..........$12.99

Jazz Hits for Piano Duet
arr. Jeremy Siskind
00143248 Correlates with HLSPL Level 5..........$20.99

Elton John
arr. Carol Klose
00296721 Correlates with HLSPL Level 5............$8.99

Joplin Ragtime Duets
arr. Fred Kern
00296771 Correlates with HLSPL Level 5............$8.99

Jerome Kern Classics
arr. Eugénie Rocherolle
00296577 Correlates with HLSPL Level 5..........$12.99

Movie Blockbusters
arr. Mona Rejino
00232850 Correlates with HLSPL Level 5..........$10.99

Pop Hits for Piano Duet
arr. Jeremy Siskind
00224734 Correlates with HLSPL Level 5..........$12.99

Sing to the King
arr. Phillip Keveren
00296808 Correlates with HLSPL Level 5............$8.99

Smash Hits
arr. Mona Rejino
00284841 Correlates with HLSPL Level 5..........$10.99

Spooky Halloween Tunes
arr. Fred Kern
00121550 Correlates with HLSPL Levels 3/4.......$9.99

Today's Hits
arr. Mona Rejino
00296646 Correlates with HLSPL Level 5............$9.99

Top Hits
arr. Jennifer and Mike Watts
00296894 Correlates with HLSPL Level 5..........$10.99

Top Piano Ballads
arr. Jennifer Watts
00197926 Correlates with HLSPL Level 5..........$10.99

You Raise Me Up
arr. Deborah Brady
00296576 Correlates with HLSPL Levels 2/3.......$7.95

HAL•LEONARD®
7777 W. BLUEMOUND RD. P.O. BOX 13819 MILWAUKEE, WI 53213

Visit our website at **www.halleonard.com**

Prices, contents and availability subject to change without notice. Prices may vary outside the U.S.